My Family

by Kelly Gaffney

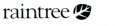
raintree
a Capstone company — publishers for children

a Capstone company — publishers for children

Raintree is an imprint of Capstone Global Library Limited, a company incorporated in England and Wales having its registered office at 264 Banbury Road, Oxford, OX2 7DY – Registered company number: 6695582

www.raintree.co.uk

Editorial credits
Marissa Kirkman, editor; Charmaine Whitman (cover), Clare Webber (interior), designers; Pamela Mitsakos, media researcher; Katy LaVigne, production specialist

Image credits
Capstone Press: Capstone Studio/Karon Dubke, cover, back cover; Dreamstime: Antoniodiaz, 8, Ron Chapple, 13; Getty Images: Karan Kapoor, 19, Studio Tec/ailead, 12; iStockphoto: AleksandarNakic, 5 bottom right, DGLimages, 15, IS_ImageSource, 7; Shutterstock: Blend Images, 9, 21 bottom, digitalskillet, 20 middle, MJTH, 17, Monkey Business Images, 1, 20 bottom right, 21 top, Odua Images, 5 middle left, pathdoc, 22-23, pixelheadphoto digitalskillet, 4, Rina_Ro, design element, Rob Marmion, 10, 11

Printed and bound in India.

ISBN: 978 1 4747 9267 7

Contents

Different families

There are many different kinds of families.
Some families have lots of children,
while others don't have any children at all.
You might live in the same house
as everyone in your family.
Someone in your family may live
a long way away.
But no matter where you live,
you are still a family.

You probably like most things
about your family.
All families have problems from time to time.
But families can also have fun together.

Here are some children who would like
to tell you about their families.

Sam's family

Hello, my name is Sam.
I live with both my parents
and my sister and brother.
My baby sister is called Emma
and my older brother's name is John.

John and I share a bedroom and have
lots of fun, most of the time.
We play football most afternoons.

John is always telling jokes when I am trying
to score.
Sometimes this makes me miss the goal!
I don't get angry with John, though,
because his jokes are really funny.

My brother, John

That's me!

Sophia's family

Hi, I'm Sophia and I am eight years old. I have an older sister called Gaby (short for Gabriella). She is sixteen.

Gaby and I live on a farm with Dad and Nana.

I really enjoy living on a farm.
We have horses, and Gaby is very good at horse riding.
I'm really excited because she is teaching me to ride my new pony.

My sister, Gaby

Sometimes I wish that I had a little brother
or sister too.
But I also enjoy being the youngest
in the family because Dad, Nana
and Gaby always make me feel special.

Nana and me

Jada's family

Hi, I'm Jada.

I live with my mum, my dad and my grandma. My grandma is my dad's mother.

Sometimes I feel a bit lonely as I don't have brothers or sisters.

But I have lots of **cousins** who often come over to visit, so there's always someone to play with.

Grandma and me

Mum, Dad and me

Feng's family

Hi, I'm Feng.
I have a mother, father
and younger brother called Hulin.

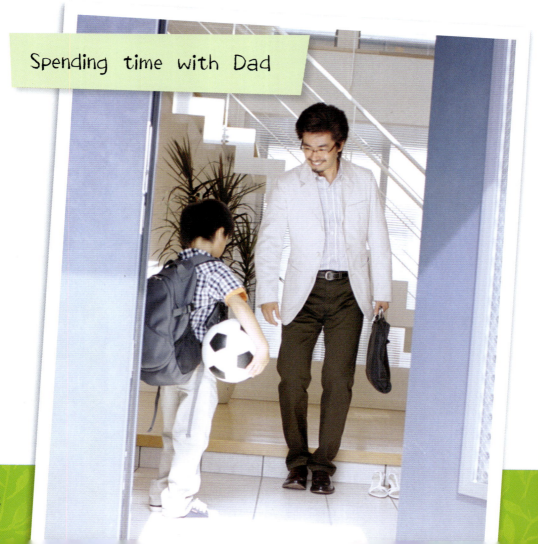

Spending time with Dad

My parents live in different houses.
I stay at my mum's house one week
and my dad's house the next.

I have to remember to pack up everything
at the end of each week.
Sometimes I find it hard, and I forget
something that I need.
But it's great spending time
with each of my parents.

Mum with my little brother, Hulin, and me

Kate's family

Hi, I'm Kate.
I have a brother called Jack.
He is my **twin**.
We are both seven years old.
We live with our two dads.

Our dads **adopted** us when we were babies.
Our family didn't start out together,
but we love each other very much.

We all help to look after our dog, Billy.
He is part of the family too!

Me, Dad, Daddy, Jack and Billy

Hana's family

Hello, I'm Hana.

I have a twin sister called Kami.

Kami and I look almost exactly the same.

Everyone always gets us mixed up.

When Kami and I sit next to each other, some people can't tell which one of us is which!

I have a very large family. My dad doesn't live with us. He and our mum are **divorced**. Our mum married another man. He is our **stepdad**. He lives with us. He has four daughters. They are our **stepsisters** and they live with us too!

My family has an enormous house with plenty of room for everyone.

That's me!

Cooking dinner with
Mum and Kami

Dev's family

Hi, I'm Dev.

I have a huge family.

I have lots of brothers and sisters,
but only my mum and dad live with me.

My brothers and sisters don't live
at home any more.

They have grown up and moved away.

They are now married and have their
own children.

Those children are my **nieces**
and **nephews**.

They come to
visit sometimes.

That's me in the middle, helping my Dad cut the cake.

All kinds of families

As you can see, there are many different kinds of families.

Some families are large, and others are small.

Families have fun together.

Who is in your family?

Glossary

adopt to become a parent of a child by law. A child may have parents who can't take care of them, so another person adopts them and becomes their parent.

cousin child of your aunt or uncle

divorce marriage break-up

enormous very big

nephew son of your brother or sister

niece daughter of your brother or sister

stepdad a man who marries a child's mother after a divorce or separation

stepsister daughter of a stepdad or stepmum

twin brothers or sisters who were born from the same mother at the same time

Index